ALL ABOUT...

ANCIENT Greece

ANNA CLAYBOURNE

Text © Anna Claybourne 2002
Editor: Liz Gogerly
Picture research: Shelley Noronha at Glass Onion Pictures
Inside design: Mark Whitchurch
Diagrams and mapwork: Peter Bull
Cover and panel artwork: John Yates

Published in Great Britain by Hodder Wayland, an imprint of Hodder Children's Books, in 2002

British Library Cataloguing in Publication Data
Claybourne, Anna
All about ancient Greece
1. Greece – History – To 146 B.C. – Juvenile literature
2. Greece – Social life and customs – Juvenile literature
I.Title II.Gogerly, Liz III.Ancient Greece
938

ISBN 0 7502 3908 5

The author and publishers thank the following for permission to reproduce their photographs: AKG 7, 9 (top), 13, 18, 27 (bottom), 29, 33 (bottom), 35 (bottom), 41, 44; Bridgeman/ National Archaeological Museum, Athens 9 (bottom), 31/ Ashmolean Museum, Oxford 10/ Ephesus Museum, Turkey 12/ Museo Archeologico Nazionale, Naples 15/ Louvre, Paris 23, 24/ Private Collection, Bonhams, London 30 (bottom)/ Institute of Oriental Studies, St. Petersburg 36/ Private Collection 37/ Museo e Gallerie Nazionali di Capodimonte, Naples 42/ Private Collection 43, 45 (top); C. M. Dixon 20, 25, 28, 30 (top), 38 (bottom), 39; Hodder Wayland Picture Library (cover), (title page), 33 (top), 35 (top); Michael Holford 8, 11, 16, 19 (top), 21, 22, 27 (top), 32, 34, 38 (top), 40, 45 (bottom); National Tourist Organization of Greece 19 (bottom)

Printed in Hong Kong by Wing King Tong Co Ltd

Hodder Children's Books
A division of Hodder Headline Limited
338 Euston Road, London
NW1 3BH

ALL ABOUT...

ANCIENT Greece

ANNA CLAYBOURNE

HODDER
Wayland

an imprint of Hodder Children's Books

TIMELINE

c. 40,000 BC *The first people settle in the area that is now Greece.*

c. 2000 BC *Rise of Minoan civilization on the island of Crete.*

c. 1500 BC *Rise of Mycenaean civilization throughout Greece.*

c. 1100 BC *Beginning of the Dark Ages.*

c. 800 BC *The poet, Homer, tells of the Trojan War.*

c. 800 BC *Beginning of the Archaic Age.*

776 BC *Date of the first Olympic Games.*

546 BC *The Persians begin attacking Greek colonies.*

c. 500 BC *Beginning of the Classical Age.*

490 BC *The Greeks defeat the Persians at the Battle of Marathon.*

480 BC *Battles of Thermopylae and Salamis.*

479 BC *The Greeks finally defeat the Persians at Plataea.*

431–404 BC *Pelponnesian Wars between Athens and Sparta.*

359 BC *Philip II comes to power in Macedonia.*

338 BC *Philip II defeats the Greeks and becomes ruler of Greece. Beginning of the Hellenistic Age.*

336 BC *Alexander the Great becomes ruler of Greece.*

323 BC *Alexander dies after creating a huge empire.*

275–146 BC *The Romans gradually conquer the Greek empire.*

In this book, the letters BC stand for 'Before Christ'. BC dates are counted backwards from the birth of Christ, so, for example, 460 BC is 10 years later than 470 BC. The letter *c.* stands for 'circa', which means 'about'.

CONTENTS

THE START OF ANCIENT GREECE

Ancient Greece is one of the most important civilizations that ever existed. The inventions, ideas and designs that came out of Greece over 2,000 years ago still have an effect on our lives today. However, ancient Greece was really several civilizations, spread out over thousands of years, hundreds of islands and dozens of different parts of mainland Greece.

This map of the Eastern Mediterranean area shows the main islands, areas and city-states in ancient Greece and the surrounding area. You may want to turn back to this map while you are reading later sections of this book.

People first moved into the area that is now Greece around 40,000 years ago. Over the centuries, they learned how to farm, make pottery and mine metals.

The Minoans flourished on the island of Crete about 4,000 years ago. They were followed by the Mycenaeans, who ruled most of the mainland. Then came the great city-states of Athens and Sparta, and the military might of the Macedonians. But, by about 150 BC, Greece had been conquered by the Romans.

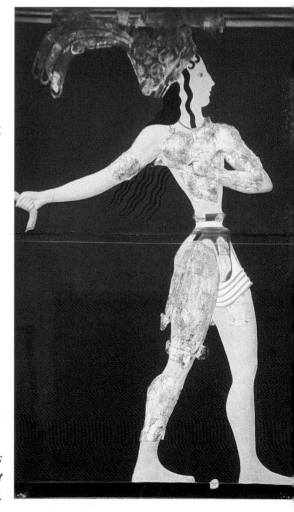

This Minoan wall painting shows a prince with a feather crown. It dates from around 1500 BC.

EARLY CULTURES

The Minoans were the first major Greek civilization. Their society was based on the island of Crete, but they were brilliant seafarers, and their pottery and sculptures have been found all over Greece. Minoan frescoes (wall paintings) show that the Minoans had large oar-driven ships, houses with several floors, a writing system, and many religious rituals. One of these involved leaping over the back of a charging bull.

This photo shows the present-day remains of the Minoans' most important palace at Knossos on Crete.

In around 1500 BC, Minoan culture began to decline. This was partly because volcanoes and earthquakes damaged Minoan palaces, and partly because the Mycenaeans invaded.

In Minoan religion, bulls were sacred. This carved bull's head was used in sacred ceremonies by priests. Minos, a famous Minoan king, was said to keep a creature called the Minotaur, which was half-man, half-bull, in a maze beneath his palace.

The Mycenaeans were the next great ancient Greek culture. They were based at Mycenae, on the mainland, and their fierce, well-equipped armies conquered almost all of Greece. They developed writing, art and architecture, and international trade with Africa, Asia and western Europe.

The Mycenaeans were great warriors, and they are also famous for their amazing gold jewellery. This bronze dagger, found in a tomb at Mycenae, is decorated with imported gold.

THE DARK AGES

Like the Minoans, the Mycenaeans eventually lost their power. Food shortages, possibly caused by earthquakes, led Mycenaean cities to raid each other for supplies. Another society, the Dorians, took advantage of this weakness, and invaded from the north.

The Dorians were less artistic than previous cultures, and many skills, including writing, were lost.

In the Dark Ages, the pictures of daily life used by the Minoans and Mycenaeans on their pots and weapons were replaced by geometric designs. This pot from Athens, with its zigzags and lines, is a good example of Dark Ages style.

Homer's poem the Odyssey *tells the story of Odysseus' long journey home from the Trojan War. This vase painting shows a scene in which Odysseus is spellbound by the beautiful voices of mysterious creatures called the Sirens.*

Most people probably lived in huts, which did not survive as ruins. Because of this, we don't know much about the time from 1100–800 BC, and it is called the Dark Ages.

The great poet Homer lived in the Dark Ages. His works, the *Iliad* and the *Odyssey*, were passed on by word of mouth instead of being written down. They tell the story of the legendary Trojan War between the Mycenaeans and the city of Troy. The Trojan War may have really happened, in about 1250 BC.

GREECE RISES AGAIN

I n around 800 BC, Greece began to emerge from the Dark Ages. Many groups of Greeks had travelled to other areas, such as Ionia (in what is now Turkey) and Italy. There they founded colonies, which began trading with each other and with the rest of Greece. This was the beginning of the Archaic Age.

This memorial stone is carved with a clear example of Archaic Greek writing. The Greeks still use a similar alphabet today, and most of Europe's modern alphabets are also derived from it.

Thanks to their trading, the Greeks grew richer, so they had more money to spend on creating beautiful buildings and artworks. They also copied many interesting design styles from the countries they had visited.

One of the countries the Greeks traded with was Phoenicia, which was roughly where Israel is now. The Phoenicians had their own alphabet, which the Greeks copied and adapted. The new Greek alphabet was easy to use, and spread quickly.

This perfume container, in the shape of an owl, comes from Corinth and dates from around 650 BC, in the Archaic Age.

CITY-STATES

Archaic Greece was made up of many city-states, such as Athens (the most important), Sparta, Corinth and Knossos. Each city-state had a main city, surrounded by walls, which ruled over the surrounding countryside. The city-states were independent and sometimes fought each other, but they all had the same Greek culture and language.

This map shows the main Greek city-states that grew up during the Archaic period, from 800–500 BC.

GREECE

Elatea

Myrina

Chalcis

Megara

Eretria

Corinth

Athens

AEGEAN

Argos

SEA

ZACHYNTHUS

Sparta

MELOS

THERA

MEDITERRANEAN

Knossos

SEA

CRETE

The Greek name for a city-state was polis, from which we get our modern word politics. All city-states had the same basic design. The walled city contained houses and other buildings arranged around a flat, open area, called the agora, which was used for markets and public meetings. A street led up to a hilltop area called the acropolis. It contained temples and statues, and was surrounded by extra-strong walls to protect the people if there was an attack.

City-states were sometimes ruled by groups of rich men called aristocrats, and sometimes by a single ruler called a tyrant. This is the tyrant Solon, who took power in Athens in 594 BC. Greek tyrants were not always evil – Solon was a kind ruler, who introduced appeal courts and encouraged craftsmen.

TRAVEL AND TRADE

The ancient Greeks walked or used horse-drawn chariots to travel around on land. However, travel by sea was vital, because Greece is made up of so many separate peninsulas and islands, and many ancient Greek colonies were across the sea.

There were no engines, so Greek ships had sails, oarsmen, or sometimes both. Ships were made of wood.

On this vase painting of a merchant sailing ship, the mast, sails and rigging are clearly visible. The figure at the end is the steersman, who is controlling the ship's direction using a rudder.

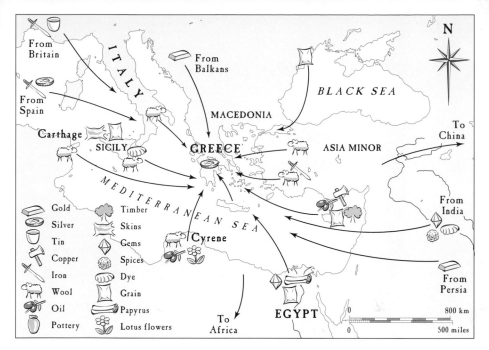

*This map shows the main Greek trading routes. Some goods, such
as gold from Persia (now called Iran), were transported over land
and sea before reaching Greece. As well as trading with other
countries, the city-states often traded with each other.*

Although they weren't very big, they covered huge
distances on trading missions to places like Egypt,
Spain, and Carthage, in North Africa.

As well as making money, trade meant the Greeks could
import materials and foods they did not have at home.
For example, they exported their wine, olive oil and
pottery around the ancient world, and imported grain,
spices and precious stones and metals.

FIGHTING FORCES

The Greeks were great soldiers. They needed military strength to conquer new lands, and to defend against attacks.

Greek foot soldiers were called hoplites. As each hoplite had to pay for his own armour and weapons, they were usually men from rich families. Armour included a body protector, a helmet with a horsehair crest, bronze greaves (leg guards), a spear, and a large round shield made of wood and bronze.

A hoplite from around 510 BC, painted on a vase from Athens. Each hoplite chose the design for the front of his own shield. It could be a painting of an animal, a scary face or a large 'evil eye'.

Hoplites marched into battle in a tight formation called a phalanx, ten to twenty men wide and up to 16 rows deep. The phalanx was so effective that Greek armies often won battles even when they were outnumbered.

For sea battles, the Greeks used fast battleships called triremes, powered by up to 170 oarsmen. A flute player played a tune to help them row in time.

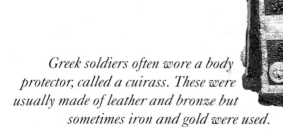

Greek soldiers often wore a body protector, called a cuirass. These were usually made of leather and bronze but sometimes iron and gold were used.

WARS WITH PERSIA

B y 550 BC, life in Archaic Greece was flourishing – but there was trouble ahead. The state of Persia (now known as Iran) began to expand, invading the lands around it. After it conquered Greece's colonies in Ionia, they fought back, and the city-states of Athens and Eretria came to their aid. This led to a series of famous battles between Greece and Persia.

Leonidas was a famous Greek commander from the city-state of Sparta. He gave his life in the battle of Thermopylae in 480 BC, when he and his men held back the Persians, allowing the rest of the Greek army to escape.

After beating Persia, the Greeks rebuilt Athens, decorating it with scenes from their successful battles. This frieze carved on a temple wall shows a Greek (on foot) and a Persian in deadly combat. Another Persian lies dead on the ground.

In 490 BC, King Darius I of Persia massed 100,000 men at Marathon, just outside Athens. However, they were beaten by just 10,000 Greek soldiers. Darius's son, King Xerxes, launched a revenge attack in 480 BC – and this time, Athens was destroyed.

A year later the Greeks made a comeback and defeated the Persians in the battles of Plataea and Mycale. Their navy surprised the Persians' ships near the island of Salamis and the Persian ships were sunk.

THE RISE OF ATHENS

After the Persian Wars, the Greek city-states made a pact to protect each other against attack. It was called the Delian League, and its most powerful member was Athens. From 479 BC onwards, this great city was rebuilt and became a centre of art, learning and politics. This period became known as the Classical Age.

You can still visit the Parthenon, a huge temple dedicated to Athene, goddess of war and wisdom and the patron goddess of Athens. It was built by a leader called Pericles in about 449 BC, as part of the rebuilding of Athens.

This is a copy of an ancient Greek statue of Athene. Her dress gives us an idea of the type of clothes ancient Greek women wore (see page 27).

Athens was known for its high culture, fashion and liberal values. This meant people were encouraged to think for themselves, and reach agreements through discussion.

Athens was also the first city-state to develop democracy – the system which allows people to vote for their leaders. It began in about 500 BC.

However, Athenian democracy was not completely fair. Women, slaves, and people from outside Athens were not 'citizens', and were not allowed to vote.

SLAVES

Ancient Greek society depended on slaves. They did many jobs, from cooking and cleaning, to playing music for parties, building, mining and farming. Not everyone could afford to keep a slave, but the family of a wealthy citizen might have several.

Some slaves were prisoners of war, taken from foreign armies during battles. Others were shipped to Greece from parts of Asia or Africa where they had been captured to order.

This bronze Greek statue from the 2nd century BC shows a slave boy from Africa. If you look closely you can see his chains.

Many citizens owned slaves completely but in some city-states, such as Athens, slaves could earn money for some tasks, and could sometimes save up enough to buy their freedom.

Drimachus was a famous slave from the island of Chios. In about 550 BC, he led a slave rebellion and many of Chios's slaves escaped to the mountains. Drimachus was later worshipped as a god of slaves.

A female slave is shown doing the cooking in this simple terracotta sculpture.

THE GREEKS AT HOME

Ancient Greek houses were usually built from stone or mud bricks, with a tiled roof. Most houses were small, but if you were rich, your house might have two floors and a courtyard.

Inside a house, there were separate spaces for men and women. Men could go out whenever they liked, and held dinner parties called symposia. But many women were expected to stay at home with their children and slaves.

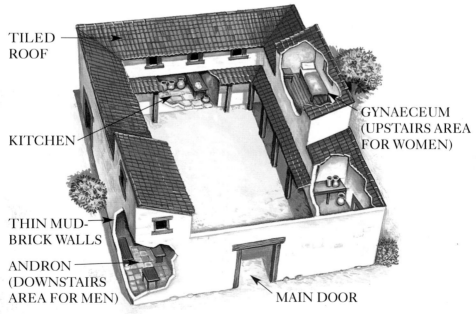

TILED ROOF

GYNAECEUM (UPSTAIRS AREA FOR WOMEN)

KITCHEN

THIN MUD-BRICK WALLS

ANDRON (DOWNSTAIRS AREA FOR MEN)

MAIN DOOR

This picture shows a Greek house with some parts cut away so you can see inside.

This vase painting from around 520 BC shows women filling their water jars at a public fountain. You can clearly see the women's tied-up hairstyles, necklaces and bracelets, and the long gowns called chitons which most Greek women wore.

Greek houses contained simple furniture, such as beds, tables and stools, and everyday items such as pots and vases. These were often painted with detailed scenes which tell us a lot about ancient Greek life.

Because they could go outside, men usually did the shopping at stalls in the agora (marketplace). However, poorer women and female servants could also go outdoors.

A group of men are having a feast, or symposium, in this marble carving from Athens. The food, such as fish, lamb, figs, grapes, cheese, and cakes made with honey, was served from small tables.

KEEPING CLEAN AND HEALTHY

The Greeks were good at keeping clean, and their cities had complex piped water and sewage systems. Some rich people had their own bathroom with a bathtub made of clay, which was emptied into an underground drain. Other people washed using a basin, or visited their town's public baths.

Another way to keep clean was to rub yourself with scented oil, which was then scraped off, bringing the dirt with it. Afterwards, people coated themselves in perfume.

This photo shows a water tank on the island of Rhodes. It was connected to clay pipes which carried water to the public fountain and the public baths at the bottom of the hill.

If they were ill, the Greeks used herbal medicines, or sometimes prayed to Asclepius, the god of medicine, to make them well again. The first ever doctor was a Greek named Hippocrates, who lived around 400 BC. He discovered that illnesses had causes and were not the work of the gods. He also set up the first medical school.

A bust of Hippocrates from the third century BC.

GROWING UP

Growing up in ancient Greece was very different for boys and for girls. People preferred boys, so female babies (as well as disabled or sickly ones) were sometimes left to die on a mountainside!

If you survived birth, however, growing up could be fun. The ancient Greeks invented many toys, such as puppets, spinning tops and yo-yos, and games including tug-of-war and draughts.

This terracotta statue shows a boy writing on a wax tablet. Letters were carved in the wax using a pointed stick called a stylus. The wax was then smoothed flat so that the tablet could be used again.

These bronze toy animals were made between 800 and 400 BC. They include a horse, a pig and a running deer.

Richer families had a special slave, called a pedagogue, to take the boys to school. There, boys learned reading, writing, mathematics, music and sports.

Girls stayed at home and learned household tasks, such as weaving. Some mothers taught their daughters to read and write. At the age of 15, girls were married, usually to much older men chosen by their parents.

This wall painting from about 1600 BC is probably Minoan. It shows two boys boxing. Throughout ancient Greek history, boys were trained to take part in sport, which was very important in Greek society (see page 32).

THE OLYMPIC GAMES

The Greeks loved sports, and every four years they held a huge sports competition in a place called Olympia. This was the ancestor of the Olympic Games which are still held today.

Men (but not women) came from all over Greece to watch and take part in the Games. They were so important that wars were called off for a few months so that people could travel safely.

This vase from Athens shows runners taking part in a race. They are just reaching a post which marks a turning point.

This is a model of Olympia, where the Greeks held a huge sports contest every four years.

This picture shows the present-day remains of the sports stadium at Olympia. You can still see the starting line for races.

The Games included running, wrestling, boxing, discus-throwing, javelin-throwing and chariot-racing. The sportsmen competed naked in a large, specially built stadium, and winners were given ribbons or wreaths of laurel leaves. There were no cash prizes, but winning brought great glory, and a successful sportsman might be rewarded by his city-state when he got home.

THEATRE AND THE ARTS

Some of the most famous writers of all time came from ancient Greece. They mostly wrote drama, since the Greeks loved going to see plays at the theatre. Over time, drama developed from a single man speaking on the stage, to the type of plays we know today, with a plot and lots of actors with different roles.

Plays could be tragedies or comedies. Tragedies usually told stories from Greek mythology, which often had unhappy endings. Comedies told fairytale-type stories or poked fun at politicians. Some ancient Greek plays, such as *Medea* by the playwright Euripides, have survived and are still performed today.

Plays were shown in huge, open-air theatres, like this one at Delphi. Some could hold over 20,000 people. It was hard to see from the back, so the actors (who were all men) often wore bright masks.

Besides the main actors, there was a chorus in each Greek play. A chorus was made up of about 15 people who danced, sang and spoke as a group. This chorus is performing on piggy back.

The Greeks also valued other arts, especially music, dancing, painting, sculpture and poetry. The leaders of city-states often encouraged artists and craftsmen, paying them to build beautiful statues and decorate temples.

This painting of a young woman with a writing tablet and stylus is said to be a picture of Sappho, a famous Greek poet. She lived from about 650–610 BC and was known for her short love poems, called lyrics.

GREEK GENIUSES

The Greeks discovered a lot about science, astronomy and philosophy. Philosophers such as Plato and Socrates ran schools where they discussed the meaning of life. Scientists, such as Aristotle, studied and described things like the stars and the human body, and tried to guess how they worked. Other Greeks were great inventors – for example, Archimedes invented several new weapons, a water pump, and a pulley for lifting objects.

This is a page from a copy of the work of a great Greek mathematician called Euclid. He made many discoveries about geometry (the science of shapes).

Pythagoras, who lived from 580–500 BC, was a mathematician and philosopher. He made mathematical discoveries which are still central to maths today. He also believed that people were reborn as animals or plants, and refused to eat beans in case they contained the souls of his dead friends.

The answers Greek thinkers came up with were not always right. For example, an early philosopher named Thales claimed the whole world was made of water. However, many Greek theories did turn out to be true. The Greeks were the first to suggest that everything was made up of tiny invisible particles (atoms), and that people had evolved from other animals, such as fish.

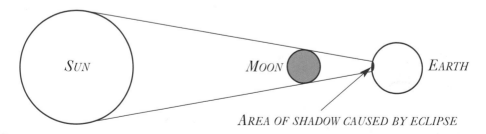

SUN   MOON   EARTH

AREA OF SHADOW CAUSED BY ECLIPSE

The Greek philosopher Thales was the first person to work out what caused an eclipse of the sun. He realized that the Earth, the Sun and the Moon must be round objects that could move around in space and cast shadows on each other.

GODS, MYTHS AND LEGENDS

T he ancient Greeks believed in many gods and goddesses. Each deity was in charge of a different aspect of the world. For example, Demeter was the goddess of crops, Apollo was the Sun god, and Athene was the goddess of war and wisdom. Zeus was the leader of the gods, who were said to live on Mount Olympus in the north of Greece.

Scenes from myths and legends were often painted on vases and carved onto temples. This vase painting shows the hero Perseus escaping with the head of Medusa, a gorgon (a type of monster) he has just killed.

In this picture, painted in Corinth in about 500 BC, you can see people leading a sheep to be sacrificed on an altar.

Each family had an altar, where they made offerings of food and sacrificed animals to their favourite gods. There were also many temples, each dedicated to a particular god or goddess.

The Greeks told many myths and legends about their gods, and about great heroes from the past.

In these stories, gods and goddesses often fell in love, argued or played tricks on each other. The gods were not seen as perfect; they had failings just like humans.

In this statue, Zeus, the king of the gods, is holding a thunderbolt and a dove. These symbolize his power to bring both disaster and peace.

THE STATE OF SPARTA

A thens was the cultural capital of ancient Greece, but the best fighters were the Spartans. The city-state of Sparta was only about 80 kilometres (50 miles) from Athens, but it was a different world. Boys were sent to training camp at the age of seven. They were taught to lie and steal, and beaten to make them tough. Girls learned wrestling and athletics to make them strong so they'd give birth to healthy babies.

This bronze statue, from the rim of a vase, is thought to show a Spartan girl athlete. Only Spartan girls wore this kind of plain, short dress. Girls from other parts of Greece had to keep their bodies covered with long gowns.

The Spartans built the toughest army in Greece, and often saved Greece from defeat. However, as the power of Athens grew, Sparta became suspicious, and in 431 BC war broke out between the two city-states. The Peloponnesian Wars raged for nearly 30 years, and Athens was seriously weakened. This paved the way for the Macedonians to invade from the north.

Sparta and Athens are both in the part of Greece known as the Peloponnese, so the wars between them became known as the Peloponnesian Wars. In this picture an Athenian politician called Alcibiades returns home after winning an important battle.

ALEXANDER THE GREAT

I n 359 BC, a leader named Philip II came to power in Macedonia, a kingdom north of Greece, and began to expand his empire. The Greek city-states formed a league against him, but in 338 BC Philip's armies defeated them and took control of Greece. This was the start of the Hellenistic Age.

In 336 BC, Philip II was murdered – perhaps by his wife Olympias. Their son, Alexander, became the next Macedonian king, and ruler of Greece, at the age of just 20. Now known as Alexander the Great, he was a heroic leader and tireless conqueror. Under Alexander, the Greeks took over parts of Persia, India and Egypt, where they founded the great city of Alexandria.

This Roman Mosaic shows Alexander's armies fighting Darius III of Persia, in 333 BC. Part of Alexander's success was due to superior Macedonian weapons, including the extra-long spears which you can see in this picture.

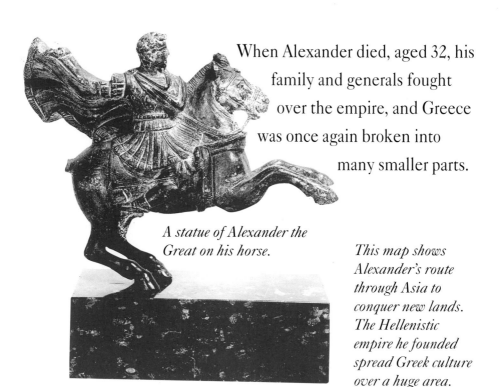

When Alexander died, aged 32, his family and generals fought over the empire, and Greece was once again broken into many smaller parts.

A statue of Alexander the Great on his horse.

This map shows Alexander's route through Asia to conquer new lands. The Hellenistic empire he founded spread Greek culture over a huge area.

THRACE

EUXINE
(BLACK SEA)

CASPIAN SEA

BACTRIA

Bactra

Granicos   Gordion

PARTHIA

Athens   Sardis
Ephesus

Issos   Arbela

Susia

IRAN

Ecbatana

MEDITERRANEAN SEA

MESOPOTAMIA

Seleucia

Tyre

Babylon   Persepolis

INDIA

Alexandria

Ammonium   Memphis

EGYPT   RED
          SEA

N

→ Alexander's route

0   1000 km

0   500 miles

THE ROMANS ARE COMING!

By about 300 BC, the Romans were becoming more powerful in and around their homeland, Italy. Their empire grew in all directions, and eventually began to threaten Greece. No longer united under a powerful leader, the different parts of Greece all fell victim to the merciless Roman armies by 146 BC.

Like the Spartans, the Romans were brutally efficient, but not very interested in art and culture. They destroyed many Greek buildings and artworks in their quest for power. However, the Romans themselves ended up being greatly influenced by Greek culture.

This mosaic shows a soldier breaking into the house of the Greek inventor Archimedes, during the Roman attack on the Greek colony of Syracuse in 212 BC. Roman soldiers were told to spare Archimedes, but they ignored their orders and killed him.

They copied Greek religious beliefs, customs, inventions and art and architecture styles, and spread them throughout the Roman empire. This is partly why so much knowledge about ancient Greece has been handed down to us today.

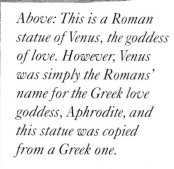

Above: This is a Roman statue of Venus, the goddess of love. However, Venus was simply the Romans' name for the Greek love goddess, Aphrodite, and this statue was copied from a Greek one.

Left: This French monument, built in 1778, shows the long-lasting influence of Greek architecture. Its steps, columns and carvings are copied from the Classical period of Greek history.

Glossary

altar *A raised platform or table used for making sacrifices or offerings to a god.*

anaesthetic *A drug used to numb pain during operations.*

architecture *The art of designing and constructing buildings.*

astronomy *The study of the stars and planets.*

citizen *A full member of an ancient Greek city-state. Women, slaves and foreigners could not be citizens.*

civilization *A complex human culture, usually with cities, art forms and religious beliefs.*

colony *A settlement controlled by another country. For example, Greece had colonies in Italy and Africa.*

empire *The area of land controlled by a particular country or ruler.*

export *To send goods (known as exports) out of a country.*

fresco *A wall painting.*

frieze *A horizontal strip of carvings, often found on the outsides of temples.*

geometric *To do with geometry, the science of regular shapes.*

import *To bring goods (known as imports) into a country.*

mosaic *A picture made up of lots of tiny tiles fitted together. The Romans often made mosaics.*

ostracize *To vote someone out of power by scratching their name on pieces of pottery. Today, to ostracize someone means to leave them out and ignore them.*

peninsula *A long finger of land sticking out into the sea.*

phalanx *A formation of soldiers arranged in tightly packed rows, often used by the ancient Greeks during battles.*

philosophy *The study of the meaning of life and the nature of things. The word philosophy comes from a Greek word meaning 'love of knowledge'.*

trireme *An ancient Greek battleship, powered by oars.*

tyrant *A leader who ruled a city-state on his own.*

INDEX